This book belongs to:
_____

A gift from:
_____

Copyright © 2022 Joan Enockson

All rights reserved. This book, or any parts, may not be reproduced in any form without written permission from the publisher.

"FINDING GEORGE" is a work of fiction. This story is original and all characters are products of the author's imagination. Any correlations to real life are purely coincidental.

"FINDING GEORGE" is Book One in the series, *Adventures on Apple Orchard Farm*.

ISBN: 978-1-958023-13-6 (Hard Cover)
ISBN: 978-1-958023-14-3 (Paperback)
ISBN: 978-1-958023-15-0 (ebook)

Library of Congress Control Number: 2022912986

Written by Joan Enockson
Cover by Abra Shirley
Illustrations by Abra Shirley

JUV001000, JUV002000, JUV002370, JUV002040, JUV002050, JUV002090, JUV002130, JUV002230, JUV039150, JUV025000, JUV039230, JUV039050, JUV039060, JUV039140, JUV039220

First printing, 2022.

Joan Enockson
Tall Girl Publishing
Laurens, IA

joanenockson.com
joanenockson6@gmail.com

FINDING GEORGE is dedicated to my cat, George. One of his eyes was injured so he likes to keep it closed most of the time. He was the inspiration for the character of George, and has been the kind of pet I have always wished for.

In 2017, my husband and I rescued George from the Almost Home Humane Society of North Central Iowa, located in Fort Dodge, Iowa. He is a very independent kitty and spends his days outside and his evenings on my lap.

FINDING GEORGE is Book One in the on going series *Adventures On Apple Orchard Farm*.

The series follows the adventures of the two main characters, Orville, the snowy white owl, and Simon, the squirrel. The two friends discover new residents, help others problem-solve, and practice what it means to be a good friend.

When I was a child, I spent the majority of my free time in the barns of my dad's dairy farm. Animals were my friends and companions. My hope for this series is that children feel connected to these characters to help them understand and nuture their own social-emotional needs.

FINDING GEORGE

Adventures on Apple Orchard Farm · Book One

Written by Joan Enockson · Illustrated by Abra Shirley

It was the middle of the night and all was dark and quiet. Orville slept peacefully on his favorite wooden rafter—that is, until he heard a strange noise.

What was that? Orville opened one eye as the feathers rose on the back of his neck. Had he actually heard something, or was he dreaming? *There it was again!* Now both eyes were wide open, his heart beating a little faster.

Orville decided it wasn't a scary noise, but it was a noise he hadn't heard before. It was a soft rustling sound, like something moving in a pile of hay. He then heard a high-pitched sound that he couldn't quite identify. He listened intently for a few minutes more, but soon the silence returned.

I'm going to find Simon in the morning and discover what those noises were. Having decided to take action when he woke up, Orville relaxed, closed his eyes, and fell back asleep.

The next morning, Orville opened his eyes to the sound of the rooster crowing.

Every morning, Big Red—the farm's red rooster—left the chicken coop just before dawn, sat on the highest fencepost, and waited for the sun to rise.

As soon as the sun appeared Big Red would lift his head, flap his wings, and blast a crow so loud it woke up the entire farm!

"Wake up, everyone, wake up!" he crowed. "The day has begun, and there's work to be done!"

At first, Orville wished that Big Red would let him sleep a bit longer, but then he remembered! *The noises! I need to find Simon so we can investigate!*

Simon's tree towered above the two-story white farmhouse. No one knew how long the old oak tree had been there, but Simon called it his home. Orville flew off his perch, swooped out the hayloft door, and headed for the giant oak tree.

Orville didn't have to wonder if Simon was awake; Simon was a very busy squirrel. He had more to do in a day than any other animal he knew! Sure enough, as soon as Orville flew toward Simon's tree, he could see him racing back and forth on a low branch, stopping quickly from time to time before racing off again.

"Simon!" Orville called. "I need your help!" Simon stopped so quickly that Orville expected him to fall over, but Simon sat straight and tall, waiting for Orville to settle in next to him.

"Good morning, Orville! Why do you need my help?" he asked in his high-pitched, excited chatter.

"I heard some strange noises last night, and I need your help to find out what they were."

"Noises? What kind of noises?"

"They were quiet sounds, but nothing like I've ever heard before. I think something or someone was near the hay mound, because I could hear the sound hay makes when it's moved or walked on. It was a light crunch, crunch, crunch." Orville thought over the events of the night before once more, remembering sitting in the dark listening to those strange new sounds. "I also heard a high-pitched sound—even higher than your voice, Simon—but I have no idea what it was."

"Hmm," said Simon, spinning the acorn he was holding with his small, nimble fingers. "You're right. We need to find out what's going on. You have sparked my curiosity, Orville. I will put this away and be right back."

Simon raced off along the branch they were sitting on, up the tree trunk, and into a hole. In no time at all, he reappeared and scurried back down to Orville.

"Let's go!" piped Simon. "I'll meet you on Raj's door."

As Simon bolted down the tree, Orville spread his wings and jumped into flight.

Orville knew Simon would get there first; he always did. It didn't bother Orville, though, because he knew that everyone was good at something, and for Simon, it was speed!

As he flew toward the barn he could see Raj, an Arabian horse, grazing in his pasture with Gary the goat by his side. They were best friends and always felt better when the other was near.

The door leading from the barn to the pasture was Raj's Dutch door. It was divided in half horizontally so the bottom half could remain shut while the top half was open. This way, Raj could look outside while he remained safe and warm in the barn. Gary, on the other hand, had to jump up and put his front hooves over the door in order to see out. He didn't mind, though, because he loved to jump! In fact, that's one of the reasons why Raj and Gary were best afriends—they both loved jumping!

Orville noticed that Simon had already reached the Dutch door, dashed up to the halfway point, and was patiently waiting for him by the time Orville landed. As they waited for their eyes to adjust to the darkened interior of the barn, Simon remarked, "This is an exciting adventure! I wonder what we'll find."

Orville replied, "I'm excited, too!"

They became quiet and listened. Suddenly, they both heard it! It was faint and seemed far away, but the sound was real!

"It's coming from the other side of the barn—let's go!" exclaimed Simon.

Before Orville could reply, Simon sprinted down the door and made his way toward the back of the barn, dodging this and that as he passed. Orville noted Simon's obstacle course of pitchforks, shovels, hay bales, grain sacks, and an oil can as he flew toward an empty five-gallon bucket. It was turned over on its end and made a perfect landing spot.

Simon leapt onto the bucket next to Orville and asked, "Do you see anything?"

Orville looked intently into the hay and replied, "No, not yet."

In the very next instant, they both saw it: a movement near the wall. "Look, over there!" cried Simon in an excited whisper, his little hand pointing in the direction of the sound. "I see something!"

 The hay moved ever so slightly to reveal one single lime-green eye. As lime-green met gold and brown, a small gray head appeared. It was a kitten! His whiskers extended beyond his rounded cheeks, and his little gray nose responded to his rapidly beating heart by flaring out with each quick breath. Orville and Simon saw that the kitten only had one eye; where the other should have been, the socket was closed and slightly sunken.

 "Hello there," said Orville, noticing that the kitten was scared. "Welcome to the hay barn. This is my friend, Simon, and I'm Orville. We'd like to be your friends, too, if you'd like."

 The kitten gently stepped out from behind the hay and replied, "I'd like that, very much."

 "What is your name?" asked Orville.

 "My name is George," he replied. "I just moved here last night with my mom, sisters, and brothers."

 "Ah," said Orville, "I heard noises last night but didn't know what they were. This morning, I asked Simon to help me investigate, and we found you!"

"We're happy to have found you and not something dangerous," Simon teased.

"Oh, no," said George with a slight purr, "I'm not dangerous."

"Why did you move to the hay barn?" Orville asked. George's face froze and his little body trembled. "I'm sorry," Orville said, "I didn't mean to upset you."

"It's okay," replied George. "I was just reminded of a bad memory."

"Yes," began Simon, jumping off the bucket to be at the same level as George. "We are your friends, and you'll always be safe with us."

Orville hopped off the bucket, too, spreading his wings briefly for balance, to stand next to Simon. George quickly crouched down when Orville extended his wings but gradually stood up as he reminded himself he was safe with his new friends.

George twitched his nose and licked a paw nervously before he began. He told Orville and Simon the story of being born in the garden shed near the hog barn, and how his mother always made sure that he and his siblings were safe, warm, and had plenty to eat.

"When our eyes finally opened and we were allowed to play outside," George continued, "my brothers, sisters, and I often went to the hog barn to play. There were lots of new piglets running around. It was fun to watch them jump, squeal, and chase each other."

George took a moment to lick his other paw before continuing. "One day, I was playing near a pen of older piglets and a very large black hog, named Boris, came up to the fence close to where I was. He said, 'Hey, furball—yeah, you with the green eye. How can anyone stand to be around you with such an ugly, deformed face! Get out of here before you get stepped on!' I didn't know what to do, or say, so I froze. I tried to move, but I couldn't.

The next thing I knew, my mom picked me up by the back of my neck and carried me back to the garden shed. She had heard what Boris said to me. I cried for a long time, but Mom never left me. She told me there will always be bullies who lash out and hurt you, but it was my job to love myself and surround myself with friends who support me. She also said that when someone says something hurtful to you, it's because they are struggling with loving themselves and are probably hurting, too."

Orville and Simon empathized with their new little friend. Orville leaned forward and said, "George, I'm so sorry that happened to you."

"Me, too," added Simon. "That was a mean thing for him to say, and I'm sure it still hurts."

"It does," replied George, "but I have a great mom, and now meeting you two helps a lot!"

"You know," mused Simon, "having one eye gives you a lot of character. It makes you unique and special. I have an idea that will make you look even more amazing than you already do!"

"What's your idea, Simon?" Orville asked, knowing that Simon usually had amazing ideas. He was looking forward to finding out what he had in mind.

George's body relaxed as he listened to Simon's kind words. Other than his mother, no one had ever thought he was amazing before.

He hoped his new friends were serious and not just making fun of him.

"Why don't you show George the barn and then meet me at Raj's door? I need to look for something."

Orville turned to George and said, "I live in this barn, too. Would you like me to show you where?"

"I would like that very much," replied George. "But first I need to ask my mom."

Before Orville could reply, George had turned around, bounded back into the hay, and disappeared.

In less than a minute, he reappeared. "I'm ready to go! As long as we stay in or near the barn, Mom said I could go with you."

"Great!" said Orville. "Do you see those stairs next to the hay mound?" George nodded. "Do you think you can climb them?"

George crouched down and raced toward the stairs, calling over his shoulder, "I love to climb!"

"I'll meet you at the top!" called Orville as he took to the air, flapping his wings hard to rise higher and higher.

The kitten looked around in wonder, his eye growing larger at the sight of the huge hayloft. Stacks of hay, in various levels, covered most of the hayloft floor. The huge bales reached up to the highest rafters along two walls of the barn.

"Wow!" marveled George, looking this way and that. "You live here?"

"Yes," said Orville, "I live here with my parents. Most of the time I like to sleep on the highest rafter in that corner." Orville extended a wing and pointed to one of the corners nearest the hayloft door. "From there, I can look out and see Simon's tree. Would you like to take a look?" George nodded and started jumping from one hay bale to the next, climbing higher and higher until he could see out the hayloft door.

Orville perched on his favorite rafter and smiled at his new friend. "Isn't it wonderful?"

George looked out over the vast expanse of the farm. He had never seen anything so beautiful in his life! Orville pointed to the giant oak tree where Simon lived and the dairy barn at the top of the hill.

"Oh, look," said Orville. "There's the garden shed where you were born."

When Orville looked over at George, he saw that his head was down. "You saw the hog barn, too, didn't you?" Orville asked gently.

George slowly nodded his head but still didn't look up. Orville thought about the pain his young friend was still feeling and remembered something his teacher had told him.

"George." George slowly lifted his head and looked at Orville. "My teacher would say that Boris is a bully. Keep reminding yourself that he has the problem, not you."

George looked at Orville. "I will try."

After taking one last look at the farm that they all called home, Orville said, "I bet Simon is waiting for us. Let's go see what fantastic idea he has come up with."

George managed to shake off his dark memories and focused on Orville's excitement. "Are all of his ideas good ones?"

"Most of them actually are!" chuckled Orville.

They made their way across the hayloft, down the stairs, and navigated the obstacle course along the barn floor to meet Simon. He was already waiting by Raj's door. His hands were behind his back and he quickly shifted his weight from one foot to the other, barely able to contain his excitement.

"There you are!" greeted Simon. "Did you enjoy the hayloft?"

George looked at Orville and said, "Yes. It was amazing!"

"Now," said Simon, "I have something even more amazing to show you!" He moved his hands from behind his back to reveal a piece of leather.

"What is that?" asked George.

"It's an eyepatch," replied Simon. "Pirates wear them when they get injured in battle. It will give your face more character and make you look tough. Would you like to try it on?'

"Oh, yes!" said George excitedly.

Simon stood behind George and gently placed the patch over the empty eye socket. He wrapped one leather strap over his head and the other across his cheek and tied it snuggly in the back.

"There," said Simon, admiring his work. "That should do it."

"Oh, wow!" beamed Orville. "That looks really good!"

Simon came around and nodded. "Anyone who wants to mess with you is going to think twice!"

"But I can't see it," George uttered as his head and shoulders drooped. He really wanted to know if what Orville and Simon were saying was true.

"I have an idea," Orville suggested. "Let's go out to Raj and Gary's water trough so you can look at your reflection."

"That's a great idea!" said Simon. "Follow me, George."

Simon led George out the barn door, around the corner, and under the fence of Raj and Gary's pasture.

Orville perched on the edge of the water trough and looked around. The trough is too high for George to look over and too smooth for him to climb up.

"How am I going to get up there?" asked George. He really wanted to see what his eyepatch looked like.

"I think I can help," said a deep voice from behind. George turned and looked up. There stood the largest and most beautiful animal he had ever seen. "Good morning. My name is Raj. Who might you be?" he asked politely.

George opened and closed his mouth several times, but nothing would come out.

"Raj," said Orville, "this is George. He and his family moved into the hay barn last night. George, this is Raj. He is a professional showjumper."

"It's nice to meet you," said Raj.

George finally found his voice and quietly replied, "It's nice to meet you, too."

"Don't forget about me!" bleated an incoming voice.

Gary, the goat, was quickly trotting over to the group. He hated being left out of any conversation. "What's going on?" he asked as he arrived.

Raj made the introductions and looked to Orville as to the reason for their visit.

Orville told Raj and Gary the story of hearing noises in the night, investigating with Simon, and discovering George. They listened intently to the story of George's encounter with Boris and how Simon had made an eyepatch for him.

"And now," said Orville, "George would like to see what the eyepatch looks like by looking at his reflection in your water trough, but we don't know how to get him up there. The trough is too high for him to look over and too smooth to climb."

"I have an idea," proposed Raj. He lowered his head down to look the small gray kitten in the eye. "Do you trust me, Patch?"

George tilted his head and said, "Patch?"

"Every professional needs a good show name. I think yours should be Patch."

Raj looked kindly at George and waited for his reply. George looked at Raj for a few moments as he thought about what Raj had said.

"I like it," George finally said, "and I trust you."

"Good," replied Raj. With his head still lowered, Raj said, "Can you jump up, grab hold of my mane, and climb up to the top of my head?"

George nodded and did just as Raj had asked. When Raj was sure the kitten was positioned safely between his ears, he slowly lifted his head and took a few steps toward the water trough. Raj then placed his head just above the water.

"Can you see now, little one?"

George looked at Raj's reflection in the water, then at himself, and finally at the eyepatch.

He turned his head this way and that to get the full effect the eyepatch had on his face. It really did add character! He now looked stronger and more confident.

George sat up a bit taller and looked at his friend. "I had no idea this would make such a difference. You guys are the best!"

He turned to look at his reflection one more time and realized that what Orville's teacher had said was right: There was nothing wrong with him. It's the bullies that have the problem. His mother, too, was right: Loving yourself and finding good friends who support you is one of the most important things in life.

Raj took a step back and lowered his head enough for George to jump off. George turned to Raj and said, "Thank you." He then looked around at all of his new friends and said, "Thank you for making me feel so welcome."

Orville flew down next to George and said, "You are most welcome, Patch."

George purred. He loved his new nickname, and he loved his new friends even more. He was going to love it here!

DISCUSSION QUESTIONS

1. What type of animal did you think was hiding in the hay when you first saw the cover?

2. Would you like to have a rooster for an alarm clock?

3. Orville and Simon are best friends. Raj and Gary are best friends. Who is your best friend?

4. Have you ever helped a friend who was sad?

5. Do you know someone that has a disability?

6. Does everyone need a friend, no matter what?

7. How can you be a better friend to someone who is alone?

8. How do you think George felt when he was sitting on top of Raj's head?

9. Have you ever looked at your reflection in water?

10. The next book is CANDACE'S BIG AUDITION. Would you like to read it?

2023

TALL GIRL PUBLISHING LIBRARY

"Just be yourself and love who you are!"

Experience the action and adventure only a snail could have!

Ages 0-8, Picture Book

Lilli wants to earn money!

Lilli learns the value of hard work, support, and sound business practices to create a successful lemonade stand business.

Ages 9-11, Chapter Book

Millie Mammoth has tiny friends that are different from her.

Join Millie as she makes a cultural difference by helping others realize that differences don't determine one's value.

Ages 0-8, Picture Book

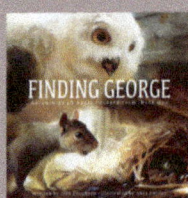

Late at night Orville hears noises, but he can't identify them.

FINDING GEORGE includes characters who show empathy for the negative effects of bullying as well as the emotional challenges of living with a disability.

Ages 7-11, Picture Book - reads like a Chapter Book

Candace doesn't know what to do!

Does she do her best, or sabotage the audition for the sake of her friend?

Look for Book Two in 2023!

Ages 7-11, Picture Book - reads like a Chapter Book

Joan Enockson is an educator, musician, and author of children's books.

Her books address social-emotional needs, friendship, citizenship, and patriotism.

She has experience teaching children of all ages in the public school system, and strives to write in a style that intrigues young readers.

Tall Girl Publishing

joanenockson.com
joanenockson6@gmail.com

George

Please leave an honest review.

Reviews help authors!

CPSIA information can be obtained
at www.ICGtesting.com
Printed in the USA
BVHW011150291222
655235BV00009B/333